"*The World Through My Eyes* offers a delightful first glimpse into the world of hummingbirds. The illustrations are beautiful; the words are simple and clear. The bright colors and the consistent theme throughout will definitely be a hit with any child. I recommend this book to both children and adults!

> ~ Judy O'Beirn, Founder & co-author of International Bestselling *Unwavering Strength* book series

The World Through My Eyes, by Igor SF Walker, tells a story of a hummingbird who wishes us to see the beauty that is everywhere. The vibrant illustrations bring this story to life, make you smile and able to see… it's all in you and me.

> ~ Jenny Jahnke, Author of *Lily Finds Hope*

Published by Hasmark Publishing, judy@hasmarkservices.com

Copyright © 2017 Igor Turkusic First Edition

No part of this book may be reproduced or transmitted in any form or by any means, electronic or mechanical, including photocopying, recording or by any information storage and retrieval system, without written permission from the author, except for the inclusion of brief quotations in a review.

Disclaimer

This book is designed to provide information and motivation to our readers. It is sold with the understanding that the publisher is not engaged to render any type of psychological, legal, or any other kind of professional advice. The content of each article is the sole expression and opinion of its author, and not necessarily that of the publisher. No warranties or guarantees are expressed or implied by the publisher's choice to include any of the content in this volume. Neither the publisher nor the individual author(s) shall be liable for any physical, psychological, emotional, financial, or commercial damages, including, but not limited to, special, incidental, consequential or other damages. Our views and rights are the same: You are responsible for your own choices, actions, and results.

Permission should be addressed in writing to SF Walker at info@sfwalker.com.

Illustrations, Ralph Becker
pyromonk@gmail.com

Cover & Book Layout, Anne Karklins
annekarklins@gmail.com

ISBN-13: 978-1-988071-68-8
ISBN-10: 1988071682

The World Through My Eyes

Follow the hummingbird on its magical journey through the wonderful sights of San Francisco.

By Igor SF Walker
Illustrated by Ralph Becker

*Dedicated to
getting things done and
enjoying what you do.*

Here's the world **through my eyes**, *at least for the next few miles.*

*I am doing this **for you**, I am not looking for a prize.*

Things I notice, ***things I see.***

All for a smile!
If everyone like that could sometimes be.

Be it a flower, a building or a tree, **beauty is everywhere**, it's in you and it's in me.

How I wish
   everyone *could see.*

All of us *in the end
the same thing share.*

*We want to put **a smile on someone's face**, because we all know and **we all care**.*

Please visit:

www.sfwalker.com

https://www.facebook.com/thesfwalker/

https://www.instagram.com/sf_walker/

About the Author

SF Walker grew up in Sarajevo during the 90s, he saw the best and the worst in humanity and the need to help others was forever ingrained into him. Walking was always a big part in dealing with that duality and he found himself walking to solutions to life's challenges everyday. He dedicated 16 years to healthcare, gaining further insight into human behavior and driving behavioral change through implementation of preventative medicine, data analytics and worksite wellness with a holistic approach. Graduating from Robbins-Madanes school for Strategic Intervention (Tony Robbins and Cloé Madanes) and specializing in helping people identify and achieve their personal goals by uncovering which human needs are the driving force behind specific behaviors, make him a great thinking partner in discovering strategies for coping with the issues that are triggering distress, anxiety, and disease.

We make your literary wish come true!

SF Walker

is excited to introduce you to his new friends

The Literary Fairies

TLF is a cool place where you can find out
how YOU could become a published author or
how to help grant a literary wish.
Have an adult visit TLF website for more details about
what we do and how you can help, and also get your
FREE colouring pages and "fill-in-the-blank story"

http://theliteraryfairies.com/free-for-kids/